Living and Nonliving

Andrea Rivera

abdopublishing.com

Published by Abdo Zoom™, PO Box 398166, Minneapolis, Minnesota 55439. Copyright © 2018 by Abdo Consulting Group, Inc. International copyrights reserved in all countries. No part of this book may be reproduced in any form without written permission from the publisher. Abdo Zoom™ is a trademark and logo of Abdo Consulting Group, Inc.

Printed in the United States of America, North Mankato, Minnesota
052017
092017

Cover Photo: Steven Schremp/iStockphoto
Steven Schremp/iStockphoto, 1; Photocreo Michal Bednarek/Shutterstock Images, 4–5; Shutterstock Images, 5, 13; iStockphoto, 6–7, 8–9, 10, 11, 12, 16, 17, 21; Lyn Gianni/iStockphoto, 15; Valentyn Volkov/iStockphoto, 18–19

Editor: Brienna Rossiter
Series Designer: Madeline Berger
Art Direction: Dorothy Toth

Publisher's Cataloging-in-Publication Data
Names: Rivera, Andrea, author.
Title: Living and nonliving / by Andrea Rivera.
Description: Minneapolis, MN : Abdo Zoom, 2018. | Series: Science concepts |
    Includes bibliographical references and index.
Identifiers: LCCN 2017931240 | ISBN 9781532120534 (lib. bdg.) |
    ISBN 978164797647 (ebook) | ISBN 978164798200 (Read-to-me ebook)
Subjects: LCSH: Life (Biology)--Juvenile literature.
Classification: DDC 570--dc23
LC record available at http://lccn.loc.gov/2017931240

Table of Contents

Science

A living thing is or was alive. There are many kinds of living things. Animals are living things.

So are plants.

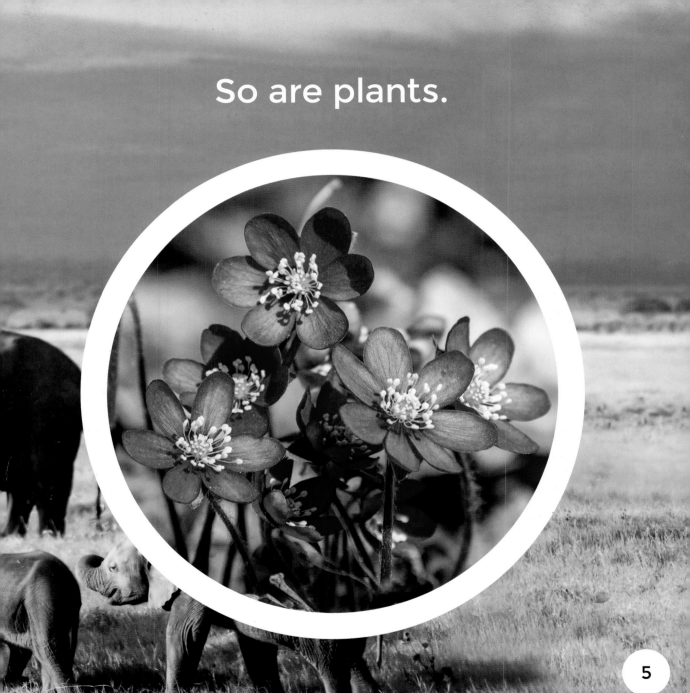

A nonliving thing has never been alive.

Rocks and clouds
are nonliving.

Technology

Many living things move. But not all things that move are alive.

Machines
can move.
But they are
not alive.

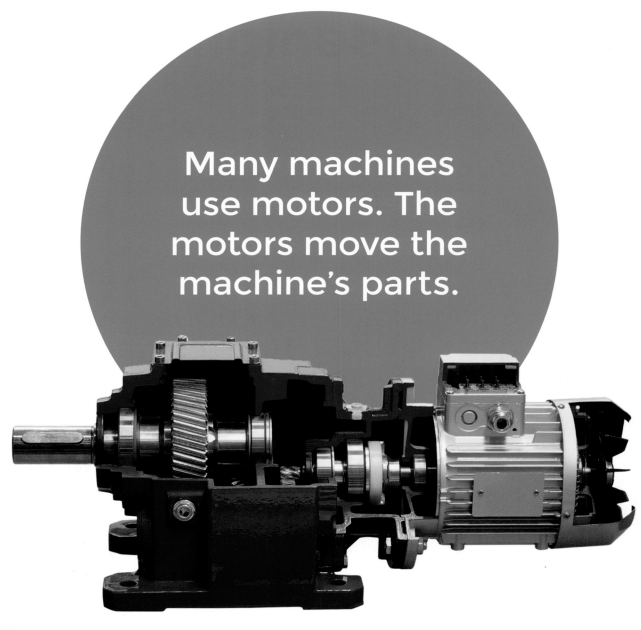

Many machines use motors. The motors move the machine's parts.

People design machines
to do many jobs.

All living things grow.
Birds grow inside of eggs.

Incubators keep eggs warm. This helps the birds inside the eggs stay alive.

Art

Chia Pets look like animals. Their bodies are made from clay. Clay is not alive. But a Chia Pet's body has seeds on it. The seeds grow into plants.

The plants are alive.

Living things grow. They breathe.

They need **energy**. They also **reproduce**. They must have all four of these **traits**.

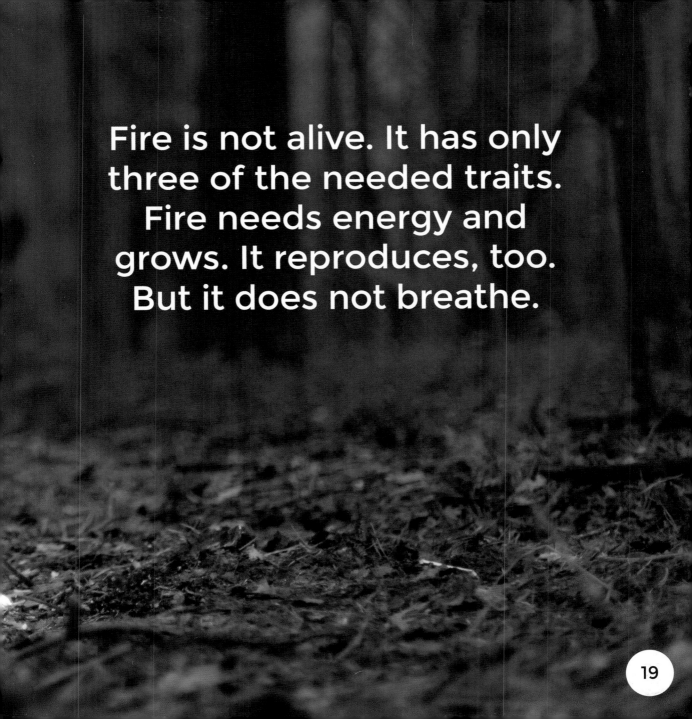

Fire is not alive. It has only three of the needed traits. Fire needs energy and grows. It reproduces, too. But it does not breathe.

- Nonliving and dead are not the same. Something is dead if it was once alive but now is not. A nonliving thing has never been alive.

- Living things respond to changes in their environments. Plants grow toward light. They bend if the light moves.

- Seeds are living things, too, since they will grow into plants.

Glossary

design - to plan how something will look or be made.

energy - power that can be used to do work, move, or grow.

incubator - a machine that is used to keep eggs warm until they hatch.

reproduce - to create another thing of the same kind.

trait - a special quality that sets a person, animal, or object apart from others.

Booklinks

For more information on
living and nonliving, please visit
abdobooklinks.com

 In on STEAM!

Learn even more with the Abdo Zoom
STEAM database. Check out
abdozoom.com for more information.

Index